FOLENS PHOTOPACK JUDAISM

David Rose

Ideas pages

Copiable pages

Folens Publishers

INTRODUCTION

Editor: Catherine Miller
Layout Artist: Suzanne Ward
Illustrations by Chris Roper

First published 1995 by Folens Limited, Dunstable and Dublin.
Folens Limited, Albert House, Apex Business Centre, Boscombe Road, Dunstable, LU5 4RL, England.

ISBN 185276 768-5

Printed in Great Britain by Gallpen Press.

This *Photopack* is a cursory introduction to one of the world's oldest monotheistic faiths. The photos have been selected to illustrate particular aspects of belief and practice, enabling the children to learn a bit more about Judaism, its thinking and expression.

The origins of Judaism are found in history more than 3000 years ago. As with the Muslim faith, Judaism is Semitic in its origins (that is, it belongs to a branch of an Afro-Asiatic family of languages which includes Arabic and Hebrew). Its beliefs and practices are an integral part of the Western world as well as feeding into both Christianity and Islam.

Throughout this *Photopack*, as a mark of respect and in line with common Jewish practice, G-d has been adopted for the name of the 'Eternal Deity'.

Spelling variations often cause concern. The spellings adopted here are those which are increasingly being used within schools in Great Britain and draw on the recommendations of the SCAA (School Curriculum and Assessment Authority) Glossary of Terms (1994).

As with most faiths there are denominational differences of interpretation regarding belief and local practice. Restrictions on space in the *Photopack* mean, therefore, that the images may not embrace all practising Jews.

The photos comprise powerful images, mostly from the author's own experiences. Some have been taken within Great Britain and others abroad.

This pack also contains an A2 poster and ten miniature reproductions of the photos. They could be used by the children as they are working on projects, for example, as a reference while researching the subject or for work in pairs. Alternatively, they could be used as the centrepiece in a collection of work in a class display.

NB: CE (Common Era) and BCE (Before Common Era) have been used in place of AD and BC as the date system in religious *Photopacks* as a mark of respect to non-Christians.

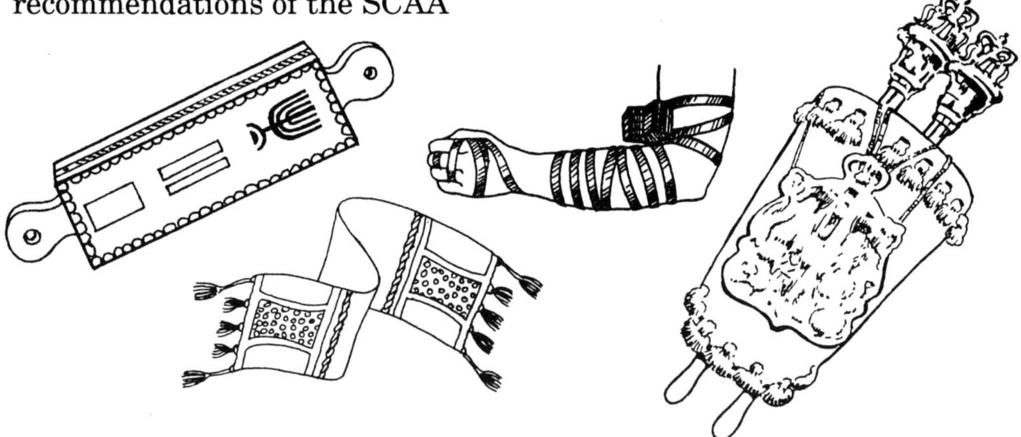

WORSHIP AND KEY BELIEFS

Photo 1

The central framework of Jewish belief revolves around the concept of the covenant relationship between G-d and the Jewish people. The Ten Commandments form the basis for this relationship and express the duty of the individual. Moses is highly revered as the person through whom G-d revealed these requirements.

Devout Jews pray three times a day, usually wearing the tallit, or prayer shawl.

The Shema is a major Jewish prayer affirming belief in one G-d and is a central credal statement which forms part of daily prayers. The Shema is contained within tefillin (small boxes containing passages from the Torah) worn on the arm and forehead; it is also placed in a small container called a mezuzah, which is placed on the entrances to Jewish homes and synagogues.

The Hasidic Jew, shown in the photo praying, illustrates the desire that the heart and mind should be attached to G-d at all times, whether in conversation, business or eating. The clothing worn, hairstyle adopted and the lifestyle followed are all symbols of this desire.

Starting points

- Ask the children to draw and label anything significant in the clothing or appearance of a male Orthodox Jew at prayer.
- Read the Shema, Deuteronomy 6:4–5. Continue to verse 9. How do the tefillin and mezuzah fulfil the requirements stated?
- The Ten Commandments in Exodus 20:1–17 are an example of religious rules for living. Discuss them and explore any other system of rules, sacred or secular.

Name of rules	People who use them
Ten Commandments	Jews and most Western countries
Five Pillars	Muslims around the world

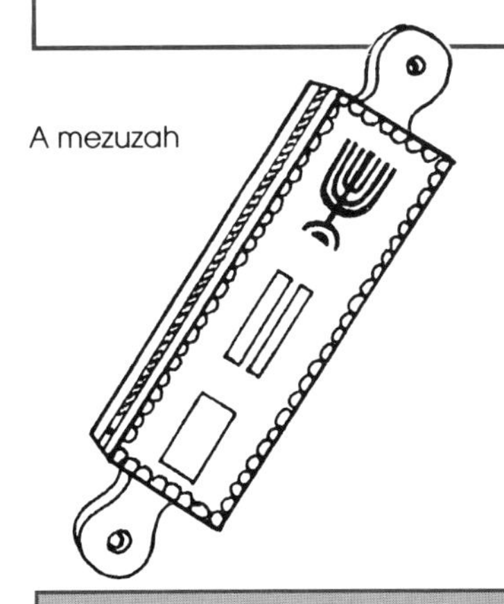
A mezuzah

Key questions

1. To which religious group does this man belong? What is he doing?
2. Is there anything special about his clothing and hairstyle? Do you know any other groups that wear special clothing?
3. Is this man somewhere special? What are the other people doing?
4. What do you think might be found in the cracks in the wall?

Activities

- Ask the children to draw two tablets with the Ten Commandments on them. Display them, along with other systems of rules from different faiths.
- Make and illustrate a set of class rules, having first discussed their value and rationale.
- Explore how rules are made, within a democracy and elsewhere, and what life would be like within a different system. Discuss what happens if people in society keep on breaking rules.
- Read the story of the Golden Calf (Exodus 32:15–20). Talk about the concept of loyalty and friendship, finding out how important this is to the children.

Themes

Law, authority, beliefs, key figures, society, democracy.

IN THE COMMUNITY

Photo 2

To have Jewish status it is necessary to have a Jewish mother (or else to convert to the faith). Consequently within Judaism there are many categories of 'Jew', from secular and atheistic through to the more commonly found Progressive and Orthodox.

The role of the mother in the home and her influence on the family should never be underestimated.

Shabbat is the seventh day of the week, the day on which G-d rested (Genesis 1). From sunset on Friday through to sunset on Saturday, Jews refrain from work and normal activity. This reflects the fifth of the Ten Commandments (Exodus 20:8–11).

It is the mother who normally leads the family into the Shabbat prayers. This involves the lighting of two candles. One represents 'remember', the other 'keep'. Having covered her eyes, the first things she sees are the flames. She then turns to her family and says 'Shabbat Shalom', meaning 'peaceful Shabbat'. These candlesticks are often given to a daughter at her Bat Mitzvah in readiness for her 'adult' role.

Many Jews endeavour to attend weekly Shabbat services at the synagogue. Prayers are said at home.

Starting points

- Research what happens within a Jewish family as Shabbat approaches and begins. How might Shabbat keep a family together? Do other religions have similar special days?
- Look at how the senses are involved with Shabbat. Try and obtain examples of the following and involve the children in actively exploring them (see the illustration below):
  sight – candles
  touch – Sefer Torah (Five Books of Moses), spice box, plaited candle
  taste – wine, cholent, challah
  hearing – songs/words of praise from a synagogue service
  smell – spice box, cholent, baking challah.

Key questions

1. What is this lady doing? Is it part of a ceremony? Is this something she might do often?
2. What objects can you see? Do they have any meaning?
3. Do you think this is an event that the family enjoys? Are there occasions at your home that all of the family join in?

Investigate the use of senses, perhaps making use of the artefacts involved with Shabbat.

Themes

Sharing, remembering, story, identity, calendar, special days, symbol.

Activities

- The children could try making challah bread for a display of a Shabbat table. (Challah bread has eggs added and is always plaited.) Ensure there are two plaited loaves.
- Read in the Bible, Exodus 16:22–35, to find out why there are always two loaves.

PLACE OF WORSHIP – THE SYNAGOGUE

Photo 3

The word synagogue means 'a coming together' or 'meeting place'. The synagogue has three main functions. It is a place where the sacred text – the Torah – is housed and where Jews pray and worship; it is a place of teaching and education; and it is a place where the community gathers together.

The synagogue (or Bet ha Knesset) has its origins in the Babylonian exile in the fifth century BCE, when the Jews were exiled from Israel (Judah) and the temple in Jerusalem destroyed.

Within the Orthodox Jewish tradition men and women worship separately, so their synagogues may have a balcony for women, or screens to separate the sexes. Progressive Jews may sit and worship together.

This photo shows the entrance to the oldest synagogue in Great Britain, the Bevis Marks synagogue in London's East End. The building dates from 1701 and was built by Sephardic Jews who had fled from persecution on the Iberian Peninsula. The interior is still predominantly lit by candles. The dual dating systems and Hebrew script can be seen above the doorway.

Starting points

- Having identified the building as a synagogue, encourage the children to discuss what it might be like inside.
- Can they think what sort of activities take place in there?
- Does any special clothing need to be worn on entry?
- With the children, list religious buildings that have rules about clothing.

Place	Clothing rule	Rule for whom?
Synagogue	Head must be covered	Men and women
Gurdwaras (Sikh place of worship)	Head must be covered Shoes must be removed	Men and women

Key questions

1. What can you identify? What clues are there about the type of building it is?
2. What dates are there?
3. What type of language or writing can you identify?

The inside of an Orthodox synagogue (see also the activity on page 15).

Activities

- Visit a synagogue. Explore the main external features first, then show the children the Ark.
- Survey local religious buildings, noting original purpose and changes.
- Research the similarities and differences between Orthodox and Reform synagogues and the way they are laid out. Illustrate as part of a wall display.

Themes

Religious buildings, symbols, local community.

FESTIVALS – PURIM

Photo 4

The theme of the festival of Purim (or Lots) is that goodness will eventually triumph over evil. It is the only festival based on a book of the Bible – the book of Esther (see the story on page 16). The account of Esther is read in the synagogue and the congregation – who may be wearing fancy dress – shout, boo and hiss at every mention of the Jewish persecutor, the villain Haman. They also use a rattle called a gregars to make a noise.

Purim is a family service and a time of rejoicing for all members of the Jewish community. This photo, of a fancy dress display, taken at the end of the Purim service, shows a group dressed up as Noah and his family, complete with umbrellas, wellingtons and a rainbow. The Ark, the receptacle in which the Torah scrolls are kept, is in the background.

Other rituals associated with Purim include a festive meal before the service, the sending of gifts of food to friends and giving money to the poor. Special foods associated with Purim include hamantaschen – triangular cookies filled with a range of foods, such as prunes and poppy seeds (see the activity on page 13).

Starting points

- Find the story of Esther in the Bible. Read some of the instructions for Purim (Esther 9:20–22) '... days of feasting and joy, days for sending presents of food to one another and gifts to the poor.' Do the children like this idea? Ask them to plan a Purim party and decide what they would include to make it special. Remember to include a banner with a Purim greeting (for instance, 'Hag Sameah – A Joyous Festival').
- The children could write their own play for Purim and perform this in assembly for the rest of the school.

Key questions

1. What do you think these people are doing?
2. The people in the centre of the photo are dressed as characters in a well-known Bible story. Do you recognise who they are?
3. Where do you think this is taking place? How can you tell? What type of writing can you see?

Activities

- Design and make a puppet show which summarises the story of Esther. Gregars could be designed and made for it.
- Discuss with the children the ways in which they are filled with hope for the future. Ask them to write a story that develops the idea of hope when things seem difficult and despair seems natural.
- Use the recipe on page 13 for making hamantaschen. More elaborate recipes can be found in the useful book for Jewish cooking, *The Gourmet's Guide to Jewish Cooking* by Carr and Obermann, published by Exeter Books.

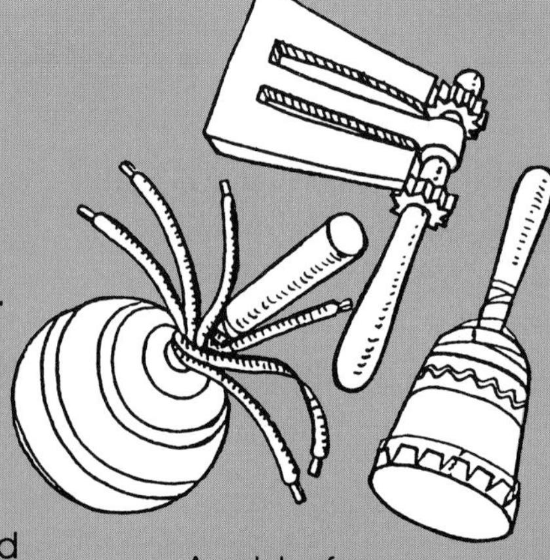

A variety of gregars.

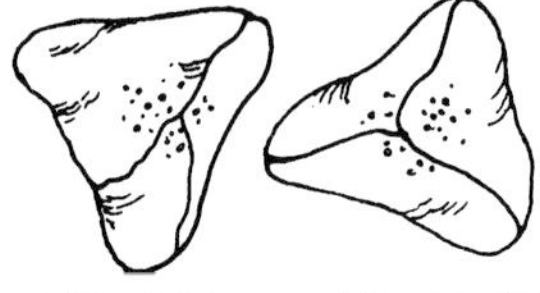

Hamantaschen – pastries traditionally eaten at Purim.

Themes

Celebration, key figures, festivals, symbols, story.

RITES OF PASSAGE – BAR MITZVAH

Photo 5

Initiation occurs at the age of 13 for Jewish boys, usually in a synagogue service called Bar Mitzvah. Bar Mitzvah means 'son of commandment'.

The equivalent for girls is 'Bat Mitzvah' (daughter of commandment) at the age of 12, which might not involve a synagogue service.

After this stage the initiate may be one of the ten adults required to form a minyan (congregation) which reads the Torah to the congregation. He also takes on the religious duties and responsibilities required of Jewish adults.

Preparation for Bar or Bat Mitzvah may have involved the learning of the Hebrew language from an early age – Bar Mitzvah is always preceded by instruction.

The initiate wears a tallit (prayer shawl), which is often a gift from his parents for the occasion. In Progressive circles the initiate may or may not wear the tefillin (boxes containing passages from the Torah) while this is the norm in Orthodox circles.

In this photo a boy performs his Bar Mitzvah in front of the Western Wall in Jerusalem. The tefillin can be seen on his forehead and left arm.

Starting points

- Do the children know what language this boy has to read? Is this a special type of book that he is reading? What language are other religious books, such as the Bible, written in?
- Ask them to consider if this is a special day for this boy. Why might it be so? What special days do the children celebrate and how do they celebrate them?

Special day	How it is celebrated
Easter	Church service/family celebrations at home.
Passing exam	Presentation at school.

Key questions

1. What is the boy wearing? What do you think he is doing?
2. What is happening to the boy?
3. What feelings do you think the boy is having?

Activities

- Ask a Jewish parent to the class – the children could interview him or her about their memories of growing up and of the regular religious routines they practised. Ask about their initiation, either Bar or Bat Mitzvah, and what it meant to them at the time and today.
- Discuss how their 'family' celebrates initiation or coming of age. Ask them to research baptism and confirmation.
- Find out about other customs of initiation in two different faiths. Concentrate on foods eaten, clothing worn, words spoken or gifts given.

The Sikh initiation ceremony of Amrit.

The Christian initiation rite of baptism.

Themes

Rites of passage, symbols, calendar, story, language, books.

SYMBOLS – THE ARK

Photo 6

The focal point in any synagogue is the Aron Hakodesh, the Holy Ark. This is a receptacle, behind a curtain called a parokhet, containing the Torah scrolls (the Five Books of Moses). The scrolls are carefully dressed and decorated in beautiful material, usually embroidered with symbolic designs. They are further decorated with a silver plate reminiscent of the type of breastplate that would have been worn by a High Priest in Biblical times. The scrolls may have a yad attached (a pointer used by the reader to avoid touching the scroll).

In front of the Ark will be the Ner Tamid, the ever-burning light which is symbolic of Shekhina (the divine presence). Phrases in Hebrew script may also be found above the Ark.

The covering on the Ark may be embroidered with symbols of Jewish identity and the faith – the Ten Commandments, the Crown (of the Torah) and the lions of the tribe of Judah.

In this photo, taken in a Reform synagogue in south west London, the three candles on either side symbolise the six days of creation and the seventh light (above, centre) is the Ner Tamid (the ever-burning light).

Starting points

- Do the children think the place in the photo is special? Encourage them to expand on their answers and broaden their scope, for instance, what places are special to the children and why?
- Ask them to research other religious occasions when lights are special, for example, Advent (Christian), Divali (Hindu), Loy Kratong (Buddhist).

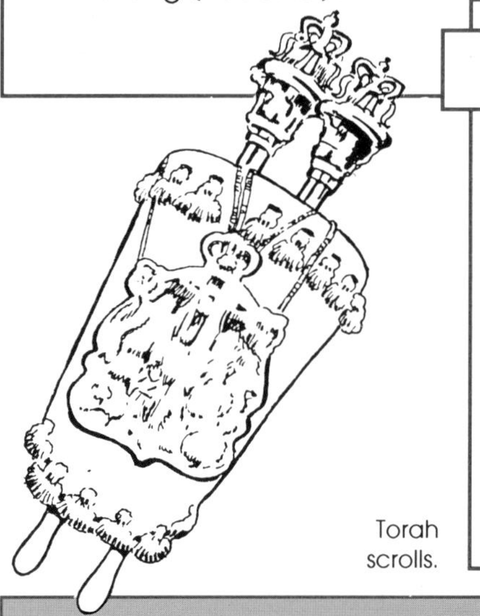

Torah scrolls.

Key questions

1. What can you see? Where might this be?
2. How many lights can you see? Does the number of lights mean anything?
3. What type of writing is in the background? Can you guess what it might say?
4. Do you think there is anything special inside the Ark? What?

Activities

- Read about the Ark of the Covenant, especially when it was first made and decorated (Exodus 37:1–16). The children research the ancient forms of measurement mentioned – the cubit mentioned in the extract, for instance, is a form of measurement based on the length of a forearm.
- Find out why the Ark in the synagogue is always on the eastern wall. Then ask the children to find out about the importance of compass directions to Muslims and to certain Christians and their churches.
- Compare how light is used in different faiths. Explore the physical examples: when flames are used, not just symbolised.

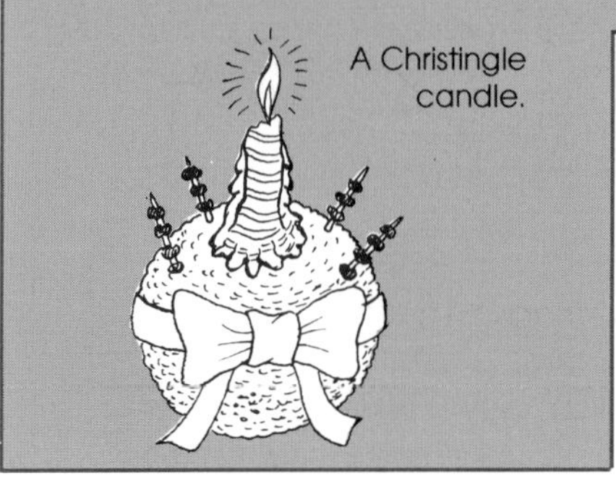

A Christingle candle.

Themes

Sacred buildings, sacred writings, symbols, sacred objects, ritual and ceremony, light, authority.

SACRED WRITINGS – THE TORAH

Photo 7

The Jewish scriptures, called Tenakh, contain three sections: the Torah, the Nevi'im, and the Ketuvim. The term Torah means 'law' or 'teaching' and contains the Five Books of Moses – Genesis, Exodus, Leviticus, Numbers and Deuteronomy. In scroll form, these parchments are kept in the Ark in the eastern part of the synagogue.

The Nevi'im (meaning 'prophets') contains the books of the prophets and historical writings, while the Ketuvim ('writings') includes books such as Psalms and Proverbs. The Torah is the most revered of the three sections.

Alongside the written Torah, an oral Torah developed. It was eventually written as the Mishnah.

This photo, taken at the North Surrey Reform Synagogue in Weybridge, illustrates their custom of unwinding the Torah scroll completely at Simchat Torah, after the last verses from Deuteronomy have been read, before rewinding to Genesis. Note the gloves worn by the congregation so that the text is untouched by the naked hand.

Starting points

- Talk about different types of scripts and the materials on which they are written.
- Find and read the story of the crossing of the Red Sea (Exodus 14).
- In groups, the children could make their own scroll on a roller, complete with a yad (pointer, often in the shape of a hand).
- Make and display a chart of the main religious writings of the world's largest religions.

Religion	Name of writing	Language of writing
Judaism	Tenakh or Torah	Hebrew
Christianity	Bible	Hebrew and Greek
Islam	Qur'an	
Sikhism		
Buddhism		

Key questions

1. In what way do you think this book is different from others?
2. Can you identify the writing?

Activities

- Look at creation stories from a range of faiths. Ask the children to create a montage.
- Look at a range of passages from the Tenakh to show different types of writings. For example, Genesis 1 – the story of creation; Psalm 23 – *The Lord is My Shepherd*; 1 Samuel 17:1–54 – the story of David and Goliath. Explore what the writers were trying to say.

Themes

Sacred writings, key figures, authority, rituals, rules, story, key beliefs, language, types of literature.

ARTEFACTS – THE MENORAH

Photo 8

The Jewish candle holder, or 'Menorah', is well known, though the number of holders varies between seven and eight. The Menorah associated with the Temple in Jerusalem had seven prongs, one for each day of the week, reminding Jews of the seven days of creation. When Herod's Temple in Jerusalem was destroyed by the Romans in 70CE, the Menorah became a symbol of hope identified with Jerusalem and its temple.

If the candle holder has nine prongs it is called a 'Hanukiah'. These candles are lit during the festival of Hanukkah, one additional candle for each day of the festival until all are lit.

Candles are used regularly in the home to symbolise the start of Shabbat, while a spice box passed around at the end of Shabbat expresses the wish for the 'aroma' of Shabbat to sustain in the coming week.

In this photo the Torah is being read from the Bimah (raised platform) in a Reform synagogue. Both the lady and the man are wearing tallits (prayer shawls). The embroidered cover on the Bimah includes the seven-pronged candlestick associated with the Temple in Jerusalem.

Starting points

- Find out about the story of Hanukkah. Discuss why the Menorah has become such an important symbol.
- On what other occasions is light used in special ways? List and display the results.

What?	When?	Why?
Lighthouse	Night-time	Warning to ships
Candles	Christmas	To represent Jesus as the light of the world
Candles	When praying at Buddhist shrine	To represent the Buddha and Enlightenment

Key questions

1. What do you think the lady is doing? What item is she holding? Why?
2. What special clothing is being worn by the man and the woman?
3. Is the candlestick embroidered on the cloth a special type?

Activities

- Ask the children to design and make a candle holder. This could be for Hanukkah candles or it could be a special birthday candle holder. Use non-inflammatory materials.
- They could design a personal symbol that somehow represents them as individuals. This could be a crest or badge.
- Write a poem on the theme of light. The verses could be written inside a candle design and then displayed.
- Research other religious artefacts, such as the tallit and tefillin. Broaden the scope to include artefacts from other religions.

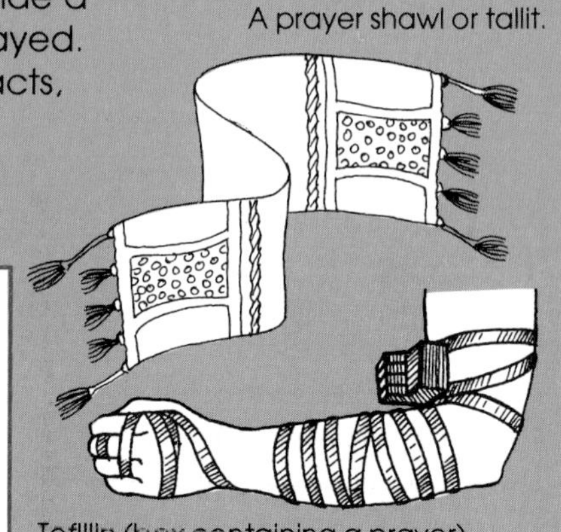

A prayer shawl or tallit.

Tefillin (box containing a prayer).

Themes

Light, writings, special clothes, celebration, symbols.

KEY FIGURES – MASTER SCRIBE

Photo 9

Scribes, or writers of the sacred texts, have always been respected for their training and scholarship. It may take 15 years before a scribe reaches a level at which they are permitted to write the Torah.

Dr Eric Ray is one of only 26 master scribes in the world today. He is a sofer – in addition to writing the Torah, he writes the texts for mezuzahs, and tefillin (see page 3).

He makes all his own ink and pens and ensures that he is ritually clean before commencing his tasks. Prayer is also important.

The sofer is not allowed to make any mistakes and checks every letter.

Much of the work of the master scribe consists of repairing old Torah scrolls. There are strict rules governing the use or non-use of a scroll. A bath, or mikveh, will be taken before the scribe writes the name of G-d and then he will use a new quill and a special bottle of ink.

The final part of writing the Torah is the stitching of the sections of parchment together. This is done by hand.

In this photo Dr Ray is inspecting scrolls for damage at the North Surrey Synagogue, in Weybridge.

Starting points

- Books, sacred or secular, may be written on a range of different materials. Research some of the materials used and illustrate a chart for display.
- Encourage the children to consider the different ways in which books can be laid out and sections assembled.

Boy reading from torah scrolls.

Key questions

1. What is this man doing? What is he wearing on his head? Why do you think he is holding a little silver pointer (a yad)?
2. Is this a special book? What type of writing is this?
3. How is this book different from other religious books such as the Bible?

Activities

- Ask the children to make their own quill pens and write a verse or passage from the Torah or Bible.
- Arrange a visit to a local synagogue so that the children can see a Torah scroll and witness how it is handled, as well as to hear what Hebrew sounds like when it is read out aloud.
- With the children's help make a list of jobs, then discuss which require long training or special preparation.

Job	Training/preparation
Vet	Years at college
Priest	Study while working
Organist	Study and lots of practise

Themes

Story, language, ritual, authority, key figure, sacred writings.

PILGRIMAGE – WESTERN WALL

Photo 10

Jerusalem is a site of religious importance that is unique. It is a place of pilgrimage for Jews, Christians and Muslims. The Western Wall in Jerusalem, often called the 'Wailing Wall', is the site of the ancient Jewish temple. There have been four temples built on the site and this photo shows the western wall of the fourth and final temple built by Herod the Great, which was destroyed by the Romans in 70CE even before it was completed.

Jerusalem, or Zion, epitomises a future of hope for Jews and forms part of Messianic expectation. Festivals such as Passover use the expression 'next year in Jerusalem' as a way of expressing confidence that G-d is acting on their behalf and that complete redemption is near.

Jewish pilgrims and worshippers congregate there. Men and women pray separately and there is a synagogue for men. Some wedge written prayers into cracks in the wall.

In this photo, the division of men and women is evident, as family groups watch their sons performing their Bar Mitzvahs. This location is considered of great significance for this rite.

Starting points

- Research the old city of Jerusalem to find out where ancient religious sites are located.
- The children could research any special journeys that any of them have made, or those that religious groups perform. Make this into a wall display or a class book, with appropriate illustrations. Photos or postcards could be added.
- Look at the Hallel psalms (Psalms 113–118) which are called the Songs of Ascents. These were sung by ancient pilgrims or those thinking about Jerusalem.

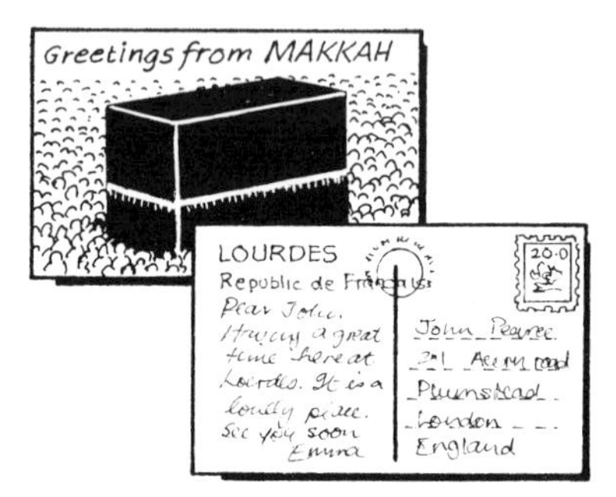

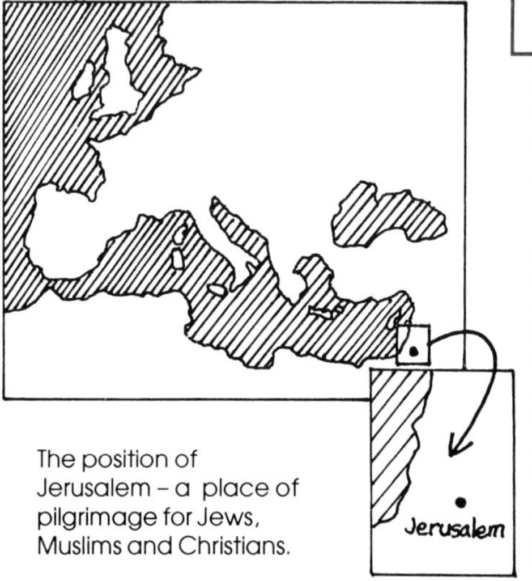

The position of Jerusalem – a place of pilgrimage for Jews, Muslims and Christians.

Key questions

1. Who can you see in this photo? Why do you think there are groups of people?
2. Where do you think it is? Is it a place of special significance? Is it special to other religions?
3. Can you suggest why Jerusalem is of great importance to Jewish people?

Activities

- Ask the children to write a letter describing their feelings to a friend, as if they were about to go on a pilgrimage or special journey, to a place where they have always wanted to go.
- They could then each write a letter to a friend as if they are a pilgrim visiting Jerusalem.
- Research and explore why Jerusalem is a place of pilgrimage for Jews, Christians and Muslims. Combine this work into a class-made book.

Themes

Pilgrimage, journeys, rite of passage, initiation, prayer, clothing.

FESTIVAL FOOD – HAMANTASCHEN

Hamantaschen are triangular pastries symbolising the ears of Haman, the villain of the Esther story (see page 16). They are filled in various ways such as with prunes or finely-grated lemon or orange rind, poppy seeds or brown beans. The recipe here uses a popular, easy-to-use mincemeat filling. It should make enough for about 25 children.

Ingredients
100g margarine
100g sugar
One egg
80g self-raising flour
80g plain flour
Mincemeat
Honey, melted
Confectioner's decorative strands

Method

1 *Cream the sugar and margarine until they are soft. Add the egg yolk and the flour to make a stiff dough.*

2 *Knead the dough lightly. Roll out until the dough is thin, then cut into 75mm rounds.*

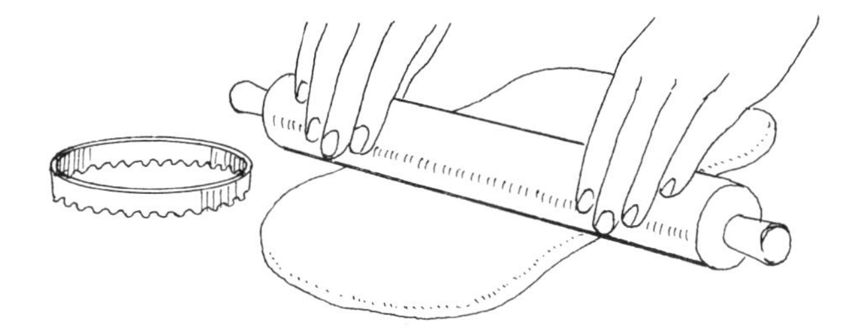

3 *Put a teaspoon of mincemeat in the centre of each round. Brush the edges with water, then take hold of the outside edges in three places, bring them up round the mincemeat and pinch them together to form triangular shapes.*

4 *Bake in the oven for 20 minutes at 220°C/425°F gas mark 7.*

5 *Brush with melted honey and sprinkle with coloured sugar strands for decoration.*

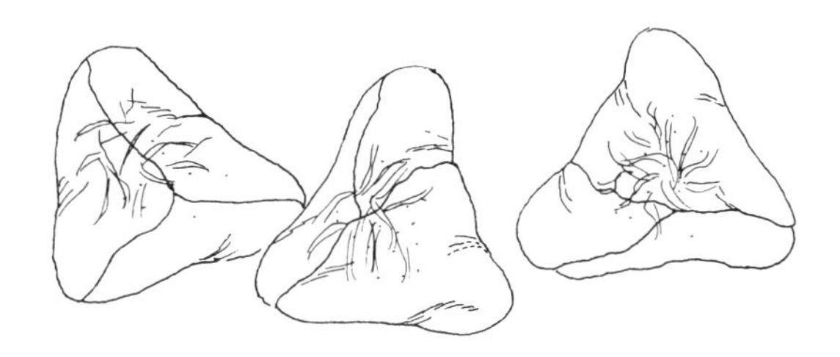

Teachers' notes (delete before copying). Make sure that the children are always carefully supervised, especially when sharp knives or heat are involved in cooking activities. Link the activity to pages 6 and 16.

JUDAISM AROUND THE WORLD

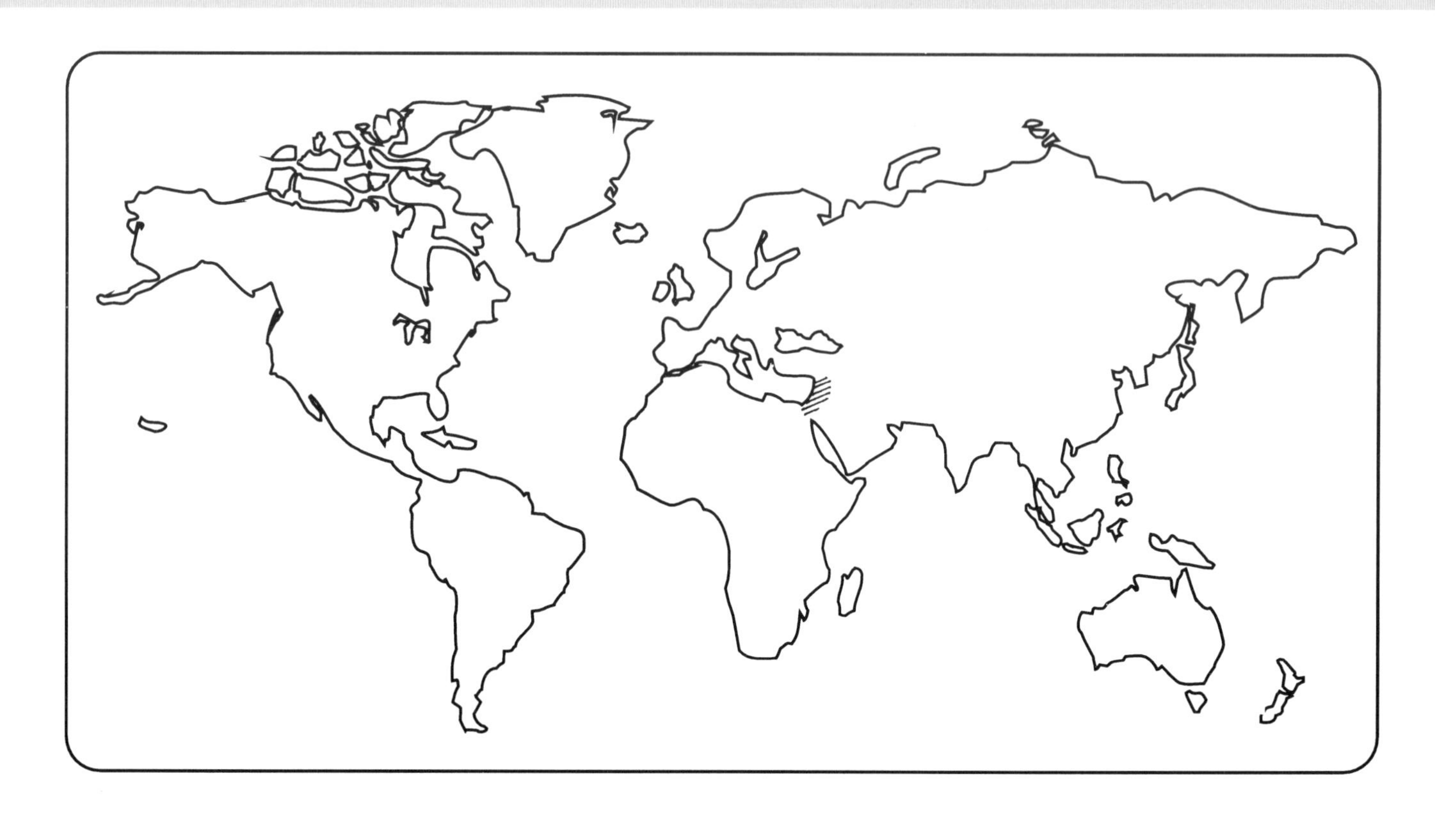

Judaism is practised all over the world, but the area marked above shows where the largest numbers of Jews practise their faith.

It is estimated that there are 12.5 million Jews in the world today, with 300 000 in Great Britain.

- Fill in the following facts about Judaism.

What do you know about Judaism?

1. The key figure who gave the Jews the Ten Commandments is the prophet ____________ .
2. The holy book of Jews is called the ____________ .
3. The special places where Jews meet and worship together are ____________ .
4. The festival when Jews celebrate the heroine Esther is called ____________ .
5. The name given to the person who writes the Torah scrolls is ____________ .
6. The name for the prayer shawl worn by Jewish men at prayer is the ____________ .
7. The most senior religious figure, or leader, in the synagogue is the ____________ .
8. The common name given to the prayer used daily by Jews is the ____________ .

TERMINOLOGY

Fill in the chart below. Some of the items are used for prayer and worship, while others are a job or items found in a synagogue.

Name and purpose	What it looks like	Suggest a similar artefact from another religion and draw it
Tallit and tzizit Prayer shawl showing the fringes (the tzizit)		
Siddur Jewish prayer book		
Bimah and Menorah A raised platform in the synagogue and a seven-branched candle holder		
Bar Mitzvah A boy's coming-of-age ceremony		
Sefer Torah A Torah scroll – the five books of Moses		
Aron Hakodesh The Holy Ark, the focal point of the synagogue		

STORY

ESTHER, PURIM HEROINE

The story of Esther is a reminder to Jews of how G-d works in unusual and unexpected ways and that He has always looked after the Jews despite persecutions. The festival is an illustration of faith and hope in G-d.

More than 2000 years ago the Middle Eastern countries were ruled over by a Persian king called Ahasuerus (Xerxes). He dismissed his first wife for disobedience. It was decided that a beauty contest should be held and whoever won it would become his new wife.

Esther, a young Jewish orphan, was persuaded by her Uncle Mordecai to enter the contest. He also persuaded her not to tell anyone she was Jewish. She won the contest and married the king.

In the meantime, King Ahasuerus had appointed a man called Haman as his prime minister. Filled with his own sense of importance, Haman demanded that everyone bow down to him when he was passing. But Jews only bow down to worship G-d and so refused to obey him.

Haman tries to make Mordecai and other Jews bow down to him.

Haman was so angry that he decided to get rid of the Jewish people. Esther's uncle, Mordecai, was one of the Jews who refused to bow down and Haman plotted to kill him. Mordecai realised that not only he, but all Jews, including Queen Esther, were at risk.

Encouraged by Mordecai, Esther braved the king's wrath by appearing before him without permission – the same sort of disobedience for which the first queen had been dismissed.

Esther braves the king's wrath by speaking to him without permission.

But the king loved Esther so much that he let her speak. She invited him and Haman to a meal with her. Haman's delight that he was important enough to be invited turned to shock when, at the meal, Esther told the king her life was in danger and someone was plotting her death. King Ahasuerus was angry and when he demanded to know who it was, Esther told him it was Haman.

Then the whole story of the plot against the Jewish people came out and in the end it was Haman who was executed, not Mordecai, and the Jewish people were saved.

This is why, at Purim every year, the Jewish people celebrate their freedom and remember the bravery of Esther many years ago.